BIOGRAPHIES

Edward Hopper

The Life of an Artist

Ray Spangenburg

Kit Moser

Enslow Publishers, Inc.

40 Industrial Road   PO Box 38
Box 398   Aldershot
Berkeley Heights, NJ 07922   Hants GU12 6BP
USA   UK

http://www.enslow.com

Edward Hopper

Library of Congress Cataloging-in-Publication Data

Spangenburg, Ray, 1939-
    Edward Hopper : the life of an artist / Ray Spangenburg and Kit Moser.
        p. cm. — (Artist biographies)
    Includes index.
    Summary: Examines the life and work of the American realist
painter, describing and giving examples of his art.
    ISBN 0-7660-1881-4
    1. Hopper, Edward, 1882-1967—Juvenile literature. 2. Artists—United States—
Biography—Juvenile literature. [1. Hopper, Edward, 1882-1967. 2. Artists.
3. Painting, American.] I. Moser, Diane, 1944-   . II. Title. III. Series: Artist biographies
(Berkeley Heights, N.J.)
    N6537.H6S66 2002
    759.13—dc21
    [B]
                                                              2002011984

Printed in the United States of America

10 9 8 7 6 5 4 3 2 1

To Our Readers: We have done our best to make sure all Internet addresses in this book were active and appropriate when we went to press. However, the author and the publisher have no control over and assume no liability for the material available on those Internet sites or on other Web sites they may link to. Any comments or suggestions can be sent by e-mail to comments@enslow.com or to the address on the back cover.

Illustration Credits: *American Artists in Photographic Portraits,* Dover Publications, Inc., 1995; pp. 9, 41; Art Resource, NY, pp. 19, 20, 31; Collection of Rev. Arthayer R. Sanborn, p. 5; Collection of Whitney Museum of American Art, New York, pp. 11, 13, 30, 35; National Portrait Gallery, Smithsonian Institute/Art Resource, NY, p. 10; *New York Then and Now,* Dover Publications, Inc., 1976, p. 17; Smithsonian American Art Museum, Washington, DC/Art Resource, NY, pp. 32, 36, 39.

Cover Illustration: Collection of Whitney Museum of American Art, New York

Contents

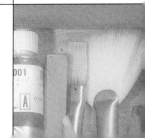

"Would-Be Artist"

Edward Hopper was famous for painting pictures that looked real. He was a tall, quiet man. He did not talk much, but he knew how to paint. He looked for scenes that showed how he felt about life. Then, he painted them. Sometimes people asked what a painting meant. He used to say, "If you could say it in words, there'd be no reason to paint." His paintings showed Americans pictures of themselves.

This photo shows Edward Hopper with his older sister Marion, in about 1890. They grew up in Nyack, New York, a small town on the Hudson River, not far from New York City.

Edward Hopper was born July 22, 1882. Marion was two years older. They grew up in the small town of Nyack, New York, on the Hudson River. Their mother, Elizabeth, was proud of her Dutch background. She was also proud of two ancestors who were artists. Edward's father, Garret Henry Hopper, had a dry goods (fabrics and clothing) store in Nyack. The business never did very well. So, the Hopper family lived with Elizabeth's mother, a widow. The house was a big, homey place on North Broadway. There was always plenty of room.

When Edward was seven, he got a blackboard for Christmas. It was great! He could draw anything on it. Then he could erase it all and draw a different picture. He practiced and practiced his drawing.

Edward took a pencil and paper along wherever he went. He drew everything he saw. He drew tents on camping trips and boats on the lake. He drew birds, horses, houses, people, and trains. He had a little paintbox, and he painted a sign on it. The sign said: "WOULD-BE ARTIST."

By the time Edward was twelve, he was already six feet tall! His classmates called him "Grasshopper" to tease him. He always spent a lot of time alone—reading and drawing.

His father thought Edward should spend more time outdoors. Edward used to go down to the harbor and watch the boats. The Nyack shipyards were famous for building racing yachts. Edward built his own boat when he was about fifteen. His father gave him the materials, but Edward did all the work. He later admitted that "it didn't sail very well."

Two years later, in 1899, Edward finished high school. By now he was strong, tall, and good-looking. He had a full, wide mouth and sharp blue eyes. He had done a lot of drawing and painting. Yet, he knew he still had a lot more to learn. He decided to study drawing in nearby New York City.

Hopper entered the New York School of Art. The famous painter William Merritt Chase taught there. Every weekday, Hopper got up early and rode the train to Hoboken, New Jersey. There, he caught a ferryboat to New York.

Edward was eager to learn. He read books suggested by his teachers. He listened carefully. At school, his teachers showed him new ways to think about art. They showed him how to put feelings and ideas in his paintings and drawings. He soon became a star student in his class.

Hopper spent seven years studying art. One teacher, Robert Henri (pronounced hen-RYE), taught him a lot. Henri said that art should tell what the artist thought and felt. Henri also said to use broad brushes—not tiny ones. He told Hopper to paint large shapes and bold pictures.

More than ever, Hopper wanted to become a great artist. He knew he was still not close to his goal. He knew he needed to find his

William Merritt Chase was an American artist who settled in New York City in 1878 and became the most important art teacher of his generation. Many of his paintings can be seen in museums around the United States.

Self-Portrait (1903). This self-portrait was drawn by Hopper in 1903, the first year that he studied under Robert Henri.

own style. To do that, he had to see more of both art and life. So, at twenty-four, he did what many other art students did in the early 1900s. He sailed for Europe.

Hopper first visited Belgium, England, Germany, and France. He visited art galleries and museums. He studied famous paintings. Finally, he arrived in Paris and stayed with a French family. Other American artists in Paris stayed up late talking, dancing, and drinking. Not Hopper. He had come to

Paris to learn about painting and drawing. Hopper liked the pale, glowing light of the French capital. Later he said, "The light was different from anything I had ever known." He drew and painted everything he saw.

Hopper returned to New York in 1907. He made two more trips to Europe. In 1909, he stayed for six months, and in 1910, he visited France and Spain. After that, he never went back.

The Railroad (1906–07, or 1909). Hopper liked to draw people in everyday life. His drawing *The Railroad* shows travelers in Paris boarding a train. He saw and drew this scene during one of his trips to Paris.

Chapter 2

Hard Times

In 1908, Hopper moved to New York. He found a way to pay the rent for a New York studio (an artist's workplace and apartment). He began doing commercial art—drawings paid for by businesses. He was good at the type of drawings used in ads and on magazine covers. He also drew pictures for stories.

Hopper hated these jobs. They took precious time away from his own paintings and drawings.

Self-Portrait (1925–1930). Edward Hopper did not do many formal self-portraits, but he often painted himself in his pictures. This self-portrait shows an ordinary looking man in a brown hat.

In those days, few of Hopper's paintings were accepted in art shows, or exhibitions. He had been busy earning money to pay the rent and did not have time to paint new pictures good enough to show. The old ones were mostly paintings he did in France. Most Americans had never been to France. They felt these pictures had nothing to do with their lives.

Finally, in 1913, two very important things happened. Hopper found a place to live in Greenwich (pronounced GREN-itch) Village. He was also asked to show his work at an important new exhibition, the 1913 Armory Show in New York.

Greenwich Village is a small neighborhood in New York. In 1913, many artists lived and worked there. Hopper moved into an apartment and studio on the top floor of a big, red brick house at 3 Washington Square North. It was a tough climb—seventy-four steps! The light up there was good for painting, though. Also, other artists lived in the building. So, even though the shy artist never spent much time with friends, he lived near other people who created art.

That same year, at the Armory Show, Hopper finally sold a painting! *Sailing,* a picture of a sailboat, sold for $250. It was a good price for a first sale—more than $4,300 in today's money. Perhaps he was moving in the right direction at last. Maybe he could stop drawing pictures for ads and live off the money from his own paintings. In fact, Hopper did not sell another painting for the next ten years. These were hard times for the tall, shy artist with big dreams.

So, in 1915, Hopper tried something different. He began doing etchings. Etchings are pictures, or "prints," made by carving a picture into a plate of metal or glass and using it with ink or paint to make pictures on paper. He could do several prints from one etching and sell them. Most artists used fancy swirls and complicated designs in their etchings, but not Hopper. His prints showed large, velvet-black areas of ink next to bright, white paper. Hopper's etchings seemed to capture a part of American life as it really was. They were direct and bold, and people liked them.

Hopper completed about sixty etchings between 1915 and 1923, but he made just a few prints of each one. After that, he stopped. More than anything else, he wanted to paint.

New York, 1911. Hopper spent most of the year in Greenwich Village in New York City.

His painting did not seem to catch on, though. In 1920, Hopper had his first solo show. Sixteen of his oil paintings hung at the Whitney Studio Club. It was a great opportunity—one of the best ways for people to learn about a new artist. Every major newspaper carried the story. A reviewer called his oil paintings "truthful and sympathetic." However, he did not make any sales.

Hopper began to paint more oils and watercolors. By the summer of 1923, his work finally began to catch on. One of his etchings won two prizes, and reviews in the newspapers were good. He sent paintings to shows in Chicago and other cities. He also spent that summer painting watercolors in Gloucester, Massachusetts. Several other artists were there that summer. Hopper knew some of them, including Josephine Nivison. "Jo" was also a former student of Robert Henri's at the New York School of Art. The two artists spent most of that summer painting together.

The Martha McKean of Wellfleet (1944). Hopper's great love and fascination with boats led him to paint many of them over the years.

Back in New York that fall, Hopper took some of his new watercolors to an art gallery. The owner told Hopper he did not like the paintings. They were "too stark," he said. By this he meant

The Lee Shore (1941). Some of Hopper's very first drawings were of the boats he saw all the time on the Hudson River near his home in Nyack, New York.

stiff, empty, and depressing. Hopper was upset. He walked out of the gallery.

Then he came to another gallery, owned by Frank Rehn. Rehn looked over the paintings. He liked them right away. He offered to take eleven of the paintings to sell. Famous collectors came to see the paintings. They liked Hopper's work. Rehn sold sixteen paintings! For the rest of Hopper's life, Rehn handled all the artist's sales.

A month later, a big art exhibition in Brooklyn showed a few of Hopper's new watercolors. They were a hit! One newspaper writer exclaimed, "What vitality and force and directness!" Things were beginning to look a lot better.

On July 9, 1924, Edward Hopper married Jo Nivison in New York. He was forty-two and she was forty-one. Hopper's place on Washington Square became their home and studio. Jo took the north end of the space for her workplace. Hopper took the south end. For heat, they had a big, old-fashioned pot-bellied stove. Every day, Hopper carried coal up the seventy-four stairs to their studio.

Hopper and his wife liked to live cheaply. They had no children, and they spent most of their time painting. The two painters knew they could not count on making a lot of money. So, they learned to stretch what money they had. They wore their clothes until they fell apart.

With the money they saved, they traveled. They went to Maine two summers in a row—then back to Gloucester in 1928. During their trips, they both painted.

Hopper and Jo were two very different people. Jo was outgoing and said what she meant.

Hopper was quiet and more polite. Jo was short and lively. Hopper was tall and awkward. They were very good friends, though, and they spent most of their time together.

Hopper continued to paint pictures of scenes along the coast. He painted lighthouses and more boats. He painted the water of the bays and inlets. He caught the way a sea breeze blows across the water. Hopper loved painting the bright summer sun. He showed the way it lit the white clapboard walls of New England houses. No one had ever before paid so much attention to these old, plain houses.

Oils, Watercolors, and Etchings

Edward Hopper painted in both oil paints and watercolors and also made prints from etchings. Most of the works shown in this book are examples of Hopper's oil paintings.

Oil paints are thick. The colors are squeezed out of a tube onto a palette. The paint might be used as thick as it is, or it might be thinned with turpentine. The artist usually mixes colors to get just the right shades. The artist can build up layers of paint and actually give texture to the painting. Oil paint is slow to dry, so the artist can scrape it off and redo sections that didn't come out quite right.

Paintings made with watercolors are more or less transparent. If the paint is applied thinly, you can see the paper right through it. The effect is more wispy and delicate looking. *Jo in Wyoming* (page 35) and *White River at Sharon* (page 36) are both watercolor paintings.

Etchings are created through a multi-step process. First, the artist carves a picture into the surface of a plate of metal. When the picture is finished, he rubs ink or paint on the plate. Then he wipes the paint off the surface of the plate. But paint remains stuck in the areas that were carved out. When the artist presses the plate onto a piece of paper, the paint comes off onto it and makes a picture. The artist can then make many identical prints using the same plate. Hopper chose to make only a few prints with each of his etchings.

Chapter 3

Motionless Movie Scenes

In January 1926, Hopper showed a new oil painting in an exhibition. Suddenly, he was a great success! Everyone was talking about *House by the Railroad.*

Like a movie director, Hopper liked to show scenes that seemed to look in on someone's life and see a story. That is what he did when he painted *House by the Railroad.* It is a simple portrait of a house. A railroad track runs in front of it. It is a powerful, emotional painting. This grand mansion seems strange. Who lives there? Why does it stand alone and silent? Is it haunted? It is like the opening scene in a movie. It seems to begin a story. Hopper lets the viewer fill in the details.

He was forty-three years old. Hopper had waited a long time for one of his paintings to make a big hit. *House by the Railroad* was the first one that really made people talk.

After that, Hopper began to paint from deep inside himself. He now knew what he wanted to "say" with his paintings. Hopper's scenes looked real. People liked the new paintings Hopper did. Some of his paintings reminded people of the countryside of their childhood. Other paintings showed city life the way it really was. For the city scenes, he used darker colors. His city scenes were sadder than his watercolors of New England. They showed that people could be lonely, even with people all around them.

Jo posed for many of Hopper's paintings. Almost every female in his paintings is Jo. Jo liked knowing she was her husband's favorite model.

Hopper showed how he felt about the city by catching it at special moments. A city is usually full of people and cars and trucks. Hopper's paintings of cities never show crowds. They show empty streets like the one in *Early Sunday Morning*. It is a picture of a business district at a time when no one is there.

"I wish I could paint more," Hopper once said. He spent lots of time sketching, especially for his oil paintings. He used yellow paper and outlined a house or scene with quick pencil lines. Sometimes, one would look especially good to him. Then he would make a painting. That did not happen often, though—only two or three times in a year! Hopper was a slow painter.

Early Sunday Morning (1930). Hopper painted this picture the year the Great Depression began. It was a hard time. Most people had very little money. *Early Sunday Morning* shows empty storefronts on an empty street. Sunday is not a shopping day. No one is even walking by or looking. There are no people—only silence.

In Hopper's city scenes, people could recognize the kinds of places where they lived and worked. Sometimes his paintings captured silent moments. People used to stop at the corner diner on the way home from work or after a movie—the way they stop today for ice cream or coffee. Hopper caught such a scene in his most famous painting, *Nighthawks,* completed in 1942.

In Hopper's painting, the ordinary people at the counter are lost in their thoughts. No one is talking. They have stopped, each one, to have a cup of coffee or a bite to eat. The minutes tick by. Hopper seems to invite us to move on. At the same time, he seems to say, "Stay for awhile."

When Hopper first began painting, movies and automobiles were new inventions. Both had a big effect on his painting. When Hopper had trouble painting, he went to the movies. When times were bad, he went to the movies three or four times a week. He loved to sit in the dark and watch the movie. Sometimes Jo would go with him, but

My Roof (1928). Not many artists would consider a simple roof to be an interesting subject for a painting. But Hopper makes you look at all the lines, shapes, and shadows in a new way.

Cape Cod Morning (1950). Not all Hopper's pictures were sad or lonely. In this painting, a woman looks forward to a new day on Cape Cod. The window frames her, but she is free. She looks out across the open field, past the shadows of the trees.

often he went alone. He looked at things the way a camera does. The pictures he painted from life were often like snapshots or scenes from a movie. Many of his pictures have the kind of lighting and point of view that we see in movies.

In 1930, Edward and Jo Hopper bought land on Cape Cod. Hopper designed a simple cottage overlooking the bay. It had a big window to let in the light for painting. The house had a special bed built extra-big for Hopper's long legs. From then on, they spent many summers there. He loved the salty air of the Cape. The sea winds reminded Hopper of his early summers in Massachusetts and Maine. He would paint all summer long.

Chapter 4

Hitting the Road!

In the 1920s, the Hoppers bought a car. It had lots of room for their easels and canvases and paints and palettes. Now they could set off down the road and travel anywhere. Hopper often returned over and over to a place he was painting. He sat inside his car and sketched. Yet, Hopper's scenes seem fresh. They look as if someone had one quick, clear look from a car window while driving by.

Hopper and Jo spent a lot of time traveling, so roads and railroads fill Hopper's paintings. Yet, his scenes show stillness. Nothing is moving. Big, empty spaces in his paintings make us want to move on down the road. Yet,

Jo in Wyoming (1946). In this watercolor painting, Hopper catches his wife, Jo, at work during a trip to Wyoming.

at the same time, they always offer an invitation to stay. The feelings in Hopper's paintings are feelings that Americans still have today. So, even though Hopper painted a long time ago, people are drawn to his paintings.

Many people thought the things he painted were ugly. Hopper painted real life—things such as little alleys, freight cars, empty train stations. He painted people drinking coffee in a restaurant. He sketched deserted streets. Most artists did not choose to paint these kinds of everyday scenes. Perhaps they did not seem "artistic" enough. Hopper found them interesting, though. So did many other people. They liked his subjects and his special style. His paintings showed people how to see what he saw.

White River at Sharon (1937). Hopper painted this watercolor work while staying at the farm of his friends in Vermont. The Hoppers had to leave there suddenly because of a rare hurricane.

The Hoppers made many summer trips. They drove across the western United States. Several times they went to Mexico. When they stopped the car, Jo and Hopper pulled out their art supplies. They sketched and painted. Jo also showed her paintings in exhibitions.

From 1941 to 1945, the United States was at war. Gasoline for the car was hard to get. So, in 1943, the Hoppers took a long train trip to get to Mexico. Later, in 1946, after the war, they were able to drive their car all the way down to Mexico. When they got there, they could not get gasoline for the car to come home! No one had told them that Mexico was still short of gas. Finally, they got some and came back. They were glad to get home, but they returned to Mexico several more times in the 1950s.

Chapter 5

The Final Years

Success took a long time to come to Edward Hopper. Once it did, the awards and honors kept on coming. In 1933, the Museum of Modern Art in New York held a retrospective exhibition—a show that looked back over all Hopper's work. Hopper thought it would be the "kiss of death." He thought everyone would think he was finished painting. He was wrong. His success and fame continued to grow.

In 1945, Hopper was elected to the National Institute of Arts and Letters. He was one of four American artists featured at the Venice Biennale, a major international exhibition in 1955. The American Academy of

Ryder's House (1933). This is the back of an old house near Ryder's Beach in Truro, Massachusetts, on Cape Cod. It is typical of Hopper to paint the back—not even the front—of an ordinary house.

Arts and Letters elected him as a member. In 1956–57, Hopper and Jo traveled to California where he was honored as artist-in-residence at the Huntington Hartford Foundation. Also in 1956, *Time* magazine put a photo of Hopper on its cover. The article was called "Silent Witness." In 1967, he was the featured artist in the United States Pavilion at the São Paulo Bienal in Brazil, another international exhibition.

During the 1950s and 1960s, Hopper was often ill and hospitalized. He painted as much as he could, but he completed fewer and fewer paintings. In the last years of his life, Hopper painted pictures that seemed to say good-bye. In *Sun in an Empty Room,* Hopper shows a room without furniture. It looks as if someone has just moved out. There are no people. There are no other objects. The sun streams in through the window, and the room is silent. His very last painting, done in 1965, is called *Two Comedians*.

On May 15, 1967, Edward Hopper died quietly in his studio in New York. He had lived in the same building for over fifty years. He was eighty-four years old. Less than a year later, Jo also died. She left most of Hopper's paintings, and many of her own, to the Whitney Museum of American Art in New York.

Hopper did not become a famous artist until he was in his early forties. He spent the early part of his career working as an illustrator. He hated the work. He was very happy when he no longer had to do it.

Since Hopper's death, museums in both the United States and Europe have celebrated his realistic scenes. Two large retrospective exhibitions have been held in recent years. In 1995, the Whitney held an exhibition called "Edward Hopper and the American Imagination." The National Museum of Art, Smithsonian Institution, in Washington, D.C., joined the Montgomery Museum of Fine Arts in Montgomery, Alabama, in a large retrospective in 1999–2000. It was called, "Edward Hopper, The Watercolors."

In her will, Hopper's wife, Jo, left all of his artwork to the Whitney Museum in New York. But you can still see many of his works on exhibit in museums all around the United States.

Timeline

1882   Born July 22 in Nyack, New York.

1889   Graduates from high school and enters art school.

1900   Begins study at the New York School of Art.

1903–04   Studies with Robert Henri.

1904   Begins teaching part-time at the New York School of Art.

1906–07   Makes his first trip to Paris.

1908   Moves to a studio in New York.

1909   Makes his second trip to Europe.

1910   Travels to Europe for the third and last time.

1913   Sells *Sailing* for $250. It is his first sale, and the last for ten years. Moves to Greenwich Village in New York.

1915–23   Works on etchings.

Timeline

1923   Paints in Gloucester, Massachusetts, in the summer.

1924   Marries Josephine Nivison on July 9. They live in New York. They paint in Gloucester during the summer.

1925   Makes his first success with *House by the Railroad.*

1930   The Hoppers buy land at Cape Cod and begin building a summer house.

1933   First Hopper retrospective, at the Museum of Modern Art, New York.

1967   Edward Hopper dies, May 15, at his studio in New York.

1968   Jo Hopper dies March 6.

Words to Know

canvas — Type of heavy cloth, stretched over a frame, that artists paint pictures on.

commercial art — Art that an artist is hired to do by a company, such as for ads.

etching — Drawing scratched onto a plate of metal, glass, or other material.

featured — Given special treatment; considered the main attraction.

ferryboat — Boat that takes people (and sometimes their cars) back and forth across a body of water.

harbor — Area of quiet waters where boats dock.

palette — Piece of wood or other surface for mixing the colors of oil paints—usually a handy size to hold.

vitality — Liveliness.

yacht — Boat used, not to earn a living, but just for the fun of boating.

Edward Hopper

Internet Addresses

The best way to learn more about any artist, including Edward Hopper, is to see the art—the real thing, not just photographs of it. That is easy if you happen to live in a large city with a large art museum, such as New York. But if you do not, try the Internet. The Web sites for Hopper listed on the next page were written for people of all ages, so the text may be a bit too hard for you to get through. That is okay, though—you are just visiting for the pictures.

An Edward Hopper Scrapbook The Smithsonian's National Museum of American Art has put together a scrapbook about Edward Hopper's life and paintings. Take a tour through his life or through his art, or both. Travel with the Hoppers on their journeys. Meet Hopper's friends. Find out about his shows and paintings.

http://nmaa-ryder.si.edu/collections/exhibits/hopper/

Artcyclopedia, The Fine Art Search Engine: Edward Hopper This site has nearly 100 links to Hopper's paintings online, as well as books and articles about him and his work.

http://www.artcyclopedia.com/artists/hopper_edward.html

Index